Nationalizing Mortgage Risk

T0268878

Nationalizing Mortgage Risk

The Growth of Fannie Mae and Freddie Mac

Peter J. Wallison and Bert Ely

The AEI Press

Publisher for the American Enterprise Institute

WASHINGTON, D.C.

2000

To order call toll free 1-800-462-6420 or 1-717-794-3800. For all other inquiries please contact the AEI Press, 1150 Seventeenth Street, N.W., Washington, D.C. 20036 or call 1-800-862-5801.

ISBN 978-0-8447-7146-5

3 5 7 9 10 8 6 4 2

THE AEI PRESS
Publisher for the American Enterprise Institute
1150 17th Street, N.W., Washington, D.C. 20036

Contents

1
Introduction

Fannie Mae and Freddie Mac are today the largest financial institutions in the United States. Many economic studies, including one by the Congressional Budget Office (CBO), have concluded that these government-sponsored enterprises (GSEs) receive an implicit government subsidy arising out of the statutory benefits they retained at the time they were "privatized" (Fannie in 1970, Freddie in the 1980s). In 1996, the CBO estimated the value of that subsidy at $6.5 billion for the previous year, and the subsidy has grown substantially larger since then.

According to the CBO, only a portion of that subsidy is actually passed along to the mortgage markets.[1] The balance, almost a third, is retained for the shareholders and managements of the two companies, accounting for more than 40 percent of their 1995 profits (which ranked them among the most profitable publicly held companies in the United States).

The lower interest rates that Fannie and Freddie can command because of their government backing permit them to out-compete any private-sector rival and to dominate any market they are permitted to enter. Although their charters are supposed to limit their activities—preventing them from competing with companies that must raise their funds without government backing—the vagueness of the charters and the political power of Fannie and Freddie have enabled them to expand with few constraints. That they can and do make soft-money political contributions, hire legions of lobbyists, and employ people with close ties to Congress as top management further ensures their insulation from scrutiny.

Meanwhile, their dominance of the residential mortgage markets grows ever greater. Reasonable projections based on statements by Franklin Raines, the chairman of Fannie Mae, suggest that, by the end of 2003, the two companies will have assumed the risk associated with almost *half* of all the residential mortgages in the United States. That means that the taxpayers, who ultimately stand behind the obligations of these two companies, will have unwittingly become responsible for almost *$3 trillion* of residential mortgage risk that should be on the books of private-sector firms.

An important decision point lies immediately ahead. As shown in this analysis, in four years, Fannie and Freddie will have either acquired for their portfolios or guaranteed more than 91 percent of all the conventional/conforming mortgages in the United States. Those are the high-quality loans on middle-class homes that have until now been virtually the only mortgages the GSEs would purchase. As they grow beyond their traditional market segment, Fannie and Freddie will have to purchase increasing amounts of lower-quality loans and hold more of those loans in portfolio, increasing their risks. If they fully hedge those risks, their extraordinary profitability will decline.

The question is whether Fannie and Freddie will (1) slow their growth to reduce the risks they take on; (2) continue their growth at the rate Franklin Raines predicted, but accept reduced profitability by hedging those risks; or (3) continue the growth in both those assets and risks in order to achieve high profitability. The evidence is that they are pursuing the third course.

To be sure, there is nothing wrong with growth, risk, or profitability. But the growth of the GSEs— aided as it is by government support—creates enormous risks for taxpayers only a decade after the savings and loan bailout, and it threatens to drive a whole sector of the private financial community out of the residential mortgage market. Those factors raise serious policy issues. The purpose of this study is to examine the implications of that growth for the mortgage market, for those who compete with Fannie and Freddie, and for the nation's taxpayers.

Chapter 2 provides background on the GSEs and the mortgage markets. It outlines the statutory links to the federal government that have led the financial markets to conclude that Fannie and Freddie will not be allowed to fail, describes the mortgage market in the United States, and summarizes both the functions and growth of the GSEs.

Chapter 3 contains detailed information on the structure of the residential mortgage market today, the growth of Fannie and Freddie's share of that market since 1995, and (if the forecasts of Fannie's chairman are correct) the share they will hold—together and separately—at the end of 2003. It shows that the GSEs' total risk—including both the mortgages they will own and those they have guaranteed—will increase from somewhat more than a third of the market today to almost half of a much larger market four years hence.

The growth of Fannie and Freddie in relation to the growth of the conventional/conforming sector of the market is examined in chapter 4. It shows that, beginning in 1998, they were already acquiring more net mortgage assets in each year than the total net principal amount of the conventional/conforming loans made in that year. The data presented in chapter 4 also show that, by the end of 1998, Fannie and Freddie were holding in portfolio or had guaranteed more than 73 percent of all conventional/conforming mortgages, and that that figure could reach almost 92 percent by 2003.

The implications of that growth are addressed in chapter 5, which discusses the possibility that—to make up for the absence of sufficient conventional/conforming mortgages—Fannie and Freddie will have to drive deeper into the subprime markets, taking more risk and displacing more of the genuine private-sector lenders who have traditionally made these loans. The chapter also discusses other financial services that Fannie and Freddie might be preparing to offer if their charters are not more strictly interpreted.

Chapter 6 continues the analysis of the implications of GSE growth, focusing on the risks to taxpayers that will be associated with the nationalization of almost half the residential mortgage market by 2003. The chapter points out that Fannie and Freddie have a choice—to hedge the greater risks they will be taking and reduce their profitability, or to maintain their level of profit growth by taking greater risk. It suggests that the incentives of management and the pressures of the financial markets will push the two GSEs toward greater risk-taking.

The study's conclusion notes that there is an inherent conflict between the GSEs' status as private, profit-making companies and the government mission they are expected to perform. There is ample evidence that their government mission is no longer necessary, and that they are using the subsidy they receive primarily to enhance their profitability and to dominate their market. Even if that were not true, the risks they are creating for taxpayers and the threat they represent to nonsubsidized private-sector competitors would argue strongly for more strictly confining them to limited areas of activity, eliminating their links to the government, or taking steps toward recapturing their subsidy through a complete privatization.

2
Background

The Federal National Mortgage Association (popularly known as Fannie Mae) and the Federal Home Loan Mortgage Corporation (Freddie Mac) are two government-chartered and government-sponsored corporations that have been assigned the statutory mission of improving liquidity in the middle-class residential mortgage markets by buying and selling residential mortgages.

Fannie Mae and Freddie Mac carry on their functions in two ways—by purchasing and holding mortgages originated by mortgage lenders, and by placing their guarantee on securities (mortgage-backed securities, or MBSs) that represent an interest in pools of mortgages they have assembled. Whether they are holding mortgage loans or MBSs in their portfolio or are guaranteeing MBSs that are then sold to investors, they are assuming the credit risk associated with those loans.

Although initially established to enhance liquidity in the mortgage markets, it is doubtful that Fannie and Freddie are necessary for that purpose today. Many private organizations are now capable of purchasing mortgages from originators and selling them—either directly or through securitization—into the capital markets. However, Fannie and Freddie now argue that they perform their public mission by reducing interest rates on the mortgages they are permitted to buy, and thus help homebuyers to obtain lower-cost financing. That claim is dubious; economists believe that the lower rates attributable to the GSEs' subsidized borrowing are simply capitalized into the cost of the homes, thus benefiting developers and homesellers rather than buyers.

Fannie and Freddie were originally government agencies but were "privatized" when they were permitted to sell shares to the public. Today, both companies are among the largest and most profitable financial institutions in the world, with their securities listed on the New York Stock Exchange.

The unusual thing about their privatization, however, is that Fannie and Freddie continue to retain a large number of connections to the government, as well as various privileges and immunities that no genuinely private company can claim:

- The president appoints up to five members (a minority) of their boards of directors.
- The secretary of the Treasury is authorized to invest up to $2.25 billion in their securities, and to approve their issuance of debt.
- They are exempt from state and local income taxes and from the requirement to register their securities with the Securities and Exchange Commission.
- Their debt securities are eligible for open-market transactions by the Federal Reserve Board and for investment by insured banks.
- Their debt securities are eligible collateral for the federal government's deposits of tax revenues in banks.
- Their securities require only a 20 percent risk-weighting (versus 100 percent for the securities and debt of private companies) under the Basel risk-based capital standards applicable to banks.

Those extraordinary advantages have convinced the capital markets that the federal government will never allow Fannie and Freddie to fail. Thus, they are able to sell their debt securities at interest rates that are consistently better than any AAA-rated corporation in the world and just slightly above the rate paid by the Treasury itself. Moreover, that favored position allows them to operate with capital levels that are much lower than those of other financial intermediaries, since the capital markets are not concerned that those low capital levels will ever mean losses to the holders of their debt or their MBSs.

The Market in Which the GSEs Operate

The residential mortgage market is composed of a number of segments—government-guaranteed Veterans Administration (VA) and Federal Housing Administration (FHA) loans; multifamily housing loans; middle-class mortgages (known as conventional/conforming mortgages, the basic loans that Fannie Mae and Freddie Mac purchase or guarantee); subprime loans (loans with credit deficiencies); home equity loans; and so-called jumbo loans, which exceed the size limit on conventional/conforming loans.

According to Federal Reserve data, FHA and VA loans constitute about 11 percent of the total market. Although similarly authoritative numbers are difficult to obtain for jumbo loans, most observers agree that those mortgages constitute another 15 percent of the market. Fannie and Freddie cannot compete for most FHA and VA loans, since those are purchased and marketed by the Government National Mortgage Association (known as Ginnie Mae), an on-budget government agency that obtains its funds at Treasury rates and thus can offer lower rates than can Fannie and Freddie.[2] Nor can Fannie and Freddie compete for jumbo mortgages, which have initial loan amounts above $252,700, the limit on the size of the loans Fannie and Freddie can purchase in the year 2000.[3]

That leaves 74 percent of the total residential market in which Fannie and Freddie can invest. Of that portion, most are conventional/conforming loans; the balance are subprime, home equity, and multifamily housing loans.

In the past, the GSEs purchased almost exclusively conventional/conforming loans, because those are the best credits available in the middle-class market. But increasingly in recent years—as they have foreseen that their need for assets will outstrip the conventional/conforming market—the GSEs have entered the market for subprime, home equity, and multifamily housing loans. Those assets are riskier middle-class credits, since they represent loans to borrowers with impaired credit (subprime loans), subordinated debt (home equity loans), and rental housing (multifamily).

GSE Growth

In a statement to a September 1999 financial conference, Franklin Raines predicted that by the end of 2003 Fannie Mae will have 28 percent of the U.S. residential mortgage market, and that its profitability will have doubled. Raines's forecast implies an 11.3 percent annual rate of growth in risk and a 15 percent annual rate of growth in profitability during 1999 and over the following four years.[4]

The Raines statement provides a valuable benchmark for assessing both the steps that Fannie Mae must take to achieve that goal and the shape of the residential mortgage market in 2003, if the goal has then been achieved.

At the end of 1999, the residential mortgage market—that is, all outstanding residential mortgage loans in the United States—had an aggregate book value of just over $5 trillion. In 1998 and 1999, that market grew strongly—by more than 8 percent each year. But its long-term growth rate has been about 6 percent. If we make the conservative assumption that the residential mortgage market will grow at that rate for the next four years, it will have a total value of about $6.4 trillion in the year 2003.

Thus, when its chairman predicts that Fannie Mae will have 28 percent of the residential mortgage market in 2003, he is saying that it will in that year have assumed the risk of mortgage loans with an aggregate value of more than $1.8 trillion. At that size, Fannie Mae may or may not be the largest financial institution in the world—depending on the size of future mergers among the world's largest banks—but it will unquestionably be the largest S&L the world has ever seen.

And in second place will be Freddie Mac, which in 1999 was about two-thirds the size of Fannie. If we assume that that relative size differential will continue through 2003, then Freddie Mac will hold in portfolio, or will have guaranteed, mortgages with an aggregate value of more than $1.2 trillion, a growth rate of 11.4 percent between 1998 and 2003.

Together, then, the GSEs in 2003 will be bearing the risk associated with more than $3 trillion in residential mortgages, or almost 48 percent of all home mortgages in the United States. The balance of the market—barely more than half—will be left to the thousands of private, nonsubsidized lenders who have traditionally provided mortgage finance in the United States.

Those extraordinary facts have a number of equally startling corollaries:

- Since the U.S. government stands behind the obligations of the GSEs, the nation's taxpayers—rather than the shareholders of private-sector mortgage lenders—will ultimately bear the risks associated with almost half of all the residential mortgage debt outstanding in the United States.
- If the total residential mortgage market is growing at 6 percent a year, and Fannie and Freddie are

growing, respectively, at 11.3 percent and 11.4 percent a year, then the GSEs cannot achieve their growth goals solely within their traditional segment of the residential mortgage market. They will have to strike out into other areas.

- The current private-sector sources of mortgage finance will be forced to consolidate and will gradually be squeezed out of the residential market; in effect, half of that sector of the economy will have been nationalized.

- Just as ominously, achieving a 15 percent annual rate of profit growth will require that Fannie and Freddie take on and retain more financial risk—in a process reminiscent of the S&L industry's ultimately fatal effort to achieve high levels of profitability only fifteen years ago.

3

Market Shares

Table 3-1 shows the growth of the residential mortgage markets since 1995. The data for the size of the FHA/VA market (line 3), multifamily mortgages (line 5), and the mortgage market as a whole (line 6), during the years 1995 through 1998, are taken from reports published by the Federal Reserve Board. Information on the size of the jumbo market (line 1) and the conventional/conforming market (line 2) was derived from industry sources. Other one-to-four-family mortgages (line 4), a residual figure, consists primarily of subprime and home equity loans. For the purpose of this study, those loans and multifamily loans (loans for apartment buildings) have been combined into a category called "all other."

Assumptions and Data

The projections for 1999 through 2003 are based on our judgment that the very strong residential real estate market during 1998 and 1999 will return gradually over the next four years to its historical pattern. Thus, although the market grew by 9.3 percent in 1998, we project that it will have grown by about 8 percent when all the data on 1999 are in, by 7 percent in 2000, and by 6 percent in each of the three years thereafter.

Historically, total residential real estate mortgage debt has grown slightly faster than nominal gross domestic product (GDP). In that context, residential mortgage debt's extraordinary growth in 1998 cannot

TABLE 3-1
SIZE OF THE RESIDENTIAL MORTGAGE MARKET, PAST, PRESENT, AND PROJECTED, 1995–2003
(dollars, in millions)

	History (Year-End)				Projection (Year-End)					Annual Growth Rate: 1995–1998 (%)	Annual Growth Rate: 1998–2003 (%)	Growth Rate Difference
	1995	1996	1997	1998	1999	2000	2001	2002	2003			
Composition of outstanding mortgage market												
1 Jumbo mortgages	568,008	602,069	639,797	699,485	755,444	808,325	856,825	908,234	962,728	7.2	6.6	−0.6
2 Conventional/conforming	1,969,096	2,087,172	2,217,961	2,424,882	2,618,873	2,802,194	2,970,326	3,148,545	3,337,458	7.2	6.6	−0.6
3 FHA/VA mortgages	466,620	497,684	525,000	524,354	546,377	566,456	584,300	602,705	621,690	4.0	3.5	−0.5
4 Other 1–4-family mortgages	505,997	532,085	572,096	673,732	747,556	818,051	883,279	952,928	1,027,281	10.0	8.8	−1.2
5 Multifamily: all kinds	277,002	294,783	310,456	340,782	368,045	393,808	417,436	442,482	469,031	7.2	6.6	−0.6
6 Total residential mortgages	3,786,723	4,013,793	4,265,310	4,663,235	5,036,294	5,388,834	5,712,164	6,054,894	6,418,188	7.2	6.6	−0.6
7 Annual growth rate (%)	4.3	6.0	6.3	9.3	8.0	7.0	6.0	6.0	6.0			

SOURCES: For all tables, historic data sources are as follows: *Federal Reserve Bulletin*, December 1999; periodic financial reports issued by Fannie Mae and Freddie Mac; and industry estimates. Projected data are the projections of Peter J. Wallison and Bert Ely.

be expected to continue. If we assume that the market will gradually return to its historic growth pattern in relation to GDP, that would reinforce the projection of a gradual return to a 6 percent growth rate beginning in 2001.

The division of the market into four subcategories—jumbo, conventional/conforming, FHA/VA, and all other (subprime, home equity, and multifamily loans)—is necessarily somewhat arbitrary. There are no official or government estimates of the size of key market segments; apart from FHA/VA and multifamily mortgages, there are no formally recognized and defined subcategories into which the market has been divided for purposes of official reporting.

Although official figures are lacking, there is a wide variety of unofficial market breakdowns.[5] The data we have received from market sources, however, indicate that jumbo loans account for about 15 percent of the market and FHA-VA loans for about 11 percent. Accordingly, conventional/conforming plus all other loans—the loans in which Fannie and Freddie can invest—account for about 74 percent.[6]

Fannie and Freddie Market Shares

Table 3–2 contains data on the respective market shares of Fannie and Freddie. The information on their shares between 1995 and 1998 was derived by comparing the information in their financial statements to known market totals. For the years after 1998, we assumed a growth rate in market shares that would permit Fannie Mae to reach the 28 percent market share projected by Franklin Raines for the year 2003. We then assumed that Freddie's growth rate would be such as to maintain its market share in relation to Fannie. That means that Fannie, which had grown at a rate of 11.2 percent annually between 1995 and 1998 (line 11), would have to grow at a slightly greater rate, 11.3 per-

TABLE 3–2
FANNIE MAE AND FREDDIE MAC MARKET SHARES, PAST, PRESENT, AND PROJECTED, 1995–2003
(dollars, in millions)

	History (Year-End)				Projection (Year-End)					Annual Growth Rate: 1995–1998 (%)	Annual Growth Rate: 1998–2003 (%)	Growth Rate Difference (%)
	1995	1996	1997	1998	1999	2000	2001	2002	2003			
Fannie/Freddie retained portfolios, total mortgages outstanding												
Fannie Mae:												
8 Retained portfolio:	252,868	286,527	316,592	415,434	528,811	635,882	754,006	877,960	1,020,492	18.0	19.7	1.7
9 Total residential (%)	6.7	7.1	7.4	8.9	10.5	11.8	13.2	14.5	15.9			
10 Conventional/conforming & all other (%)	9.2	9.8	10.2	12.1	14.2	15.8	17.7	19.3	21.1			
11 Retained + guaranteed:	766,098	834,700	895,730	1,052,577	1,208,711	1,347,209	1,485,163	1,634,821	1,797,093	11.2	11.3	0.1
12 Total residential (%)	20.2	20.8	20.9	22.5	24.0	25.0	26.0	27.0	28.0			
13 Conventional/conforming & all other (%)	27.8	28.6	28.9	30.6	32.4	33.6	34.8	36.0	37.2			

Freddie Mac:

14	Retained portfolio:	107,706	137,826	164,543	255,670	337,432	420,329	506,383	605,489	712,419	33.4	22.7	-10.7
15	Total residential (%)	2.8	3.4	3.8	5.5	6.7	7.8	8.9	10.0	11.1			
16	Conventional/conforming & all other (%)	3.9	4.7	5.3	7.4	9.0	10.5	11.9	13.3	14.7			
17	Retained + guaranteed:	566,751	610,891	640,528	734,021	846,097	943,046	1,039,614	1,144,375	1,257,965	9.0	11.4	2.4
18	Total residential (%)	15.0	15.2	15.0	15.7	16.8	17.5	18.2	18.9	19.6			
19	Conventional/conforming & all other (%)	20.6	21.0	20.7	21.3	22.7	23.5	24.3	25.2	26.0			

Fannie + Freddie:

20	Retained portfolio:	360,574	494,353	481,135	671,104	866,243	1,056,212	1,262,388	1,483,449	1,732,911	23.0	20.9	-2.1
21	Total residential (%)	9.5	10.6	11.2	14.3	17.2	19.6	22.1	24.5	27.0			
22	Conventional/conforming & all other (%)	13.1	14.6	15.5	19.5	23.2	26.3	29.6	32.6	35.9			
23	Retained + guaranteed:	1,332,849	1,445,591	1,536,258	1,786,598	2,054,808	2,290,255	2,524,777	2,779,196	3,055,057	10.3	11.3	1.1
24	Total residential (%)	35.2	35.9	35.9	38.2	40.8	42.5	44.2	45.9	47.6			
25	Conventional/conforming & all other (%)	48.4	49.6	49.5	51.9	55.0	57.1	59.1	61.2	63.2			
26	Conventional/conforming only (%)	67.7	69.3	69.3	73.7	78.5	81.7	85.0	88.3	91.5			

cent, from 1999 through 2003, and that Freddie would have to increase its growth rate from 9 percent to 11.4 percent (line 17).

Table 3–2 displays market share data in two ways: (1) the respective mortgage portfolios of Fannie and Freddie as a percentage of the market as a whole, and (2) those mortgage portfolios plus the principal amount of the mortgage-backed securities that Fannie and Freddie have guaranteed—again, as a percentage of the market as a whole. We show those data separately for two reasons.

First, while there is no significant difference between the credit risk of guaranteeing MBSs and the risk of holding whole mortgages, there is a substantial difference in profitability. Fannie and Freddie earn considerably more from retaining mortgages in their portfolios than from receiving guarantee fees on MBSs. That is because they assume an additional risk— interest-rate risk—when they retain mortgages. Accordingly, as Fannie strives to meet Franklin Raines's forecast of 15 percent annual profitability growth, we would expect to see greater proportional growth in its mortgage portfolio than in its guarantees of MBSs.[7] That differential is reflected in our projections.

Indeed, just such a trend is visible between 1995 and 1998, when Fannie's mortgage portfolio grew by 18 percent (line 8), while its total risk (mortgages plus MBSs it had guaranteed) increased by only 11.2 percent (line 11). We believe that trend will continue and will become more pronounced from 1999 to 2003, with Fannie's portfolio of mortgages increasing by 19.7 percent on an annualized basis during that period.

We project a different trend for Freddie, which (starting at a much lower base than Fannie) grew its portfolio at the unsustainable rate of 33.4 percent annually between 1995 and 1998. Since we are assuming that for 1999 and the next four years Freddie will remain about two-thirds the size of Fannie, we are projecting that Freddie will reduce the rate of growth of its retained mortgage portfolio to 22.7 percent (line 14)—a rate that will still be higher than Fannie's but will bring Freddie in 2003 to a position at which its retained mortgage portfolio will be roughly 70 percent the size of Fannie's.

Second, making a distinction between mortgages retained in portfolio and mortgages guaranteed through MBSs reveals that Fannie and Freddie have only a limited range of options available to them. When Franklin Raines predicted that Fannie Mae would reach 28 percent of the total residential mortgage market in 2003 (line 12), he could have been referring to substantial growth in Fannie's issuance of MBSs, with much lower growth in the company's mortgage portfolio. However, when he forecast that Fannie would double its profitability during that period, he could only have been talking about a substantial increase in Fannie's mortgage portfolio, since only by enlarging that portfolio can a 28 percent market share be consistent with a 15 percent year-over-year rate of profit growth.

Fannie's options are further limited by the fact that the GSEs are permitted to purchase or guarantee only those mortgages with an initial principal amount that (in 2000) does not exceed $252,700. As noted above, that limitation essentially confines them to 74 percent of the total residential market, which for ease of reference we shall call the middle-class mortgage market. Accordingly, table 3–2 also shows the growth in the GSEs' risk (mortgages and MBSs) as a proportion of that market.

Those data indicate that by 2003, Fannie is likely to hold in its portfolio 21 percent of all mortgages in that segment (line 10), and it will have assumed the risk (through holding mortgages in its portfolio or guaranteeing MBSs) of 37 percent of that market (line 13). In that same year, Fannie and Freddie together will hold in their portfolios about 36 percent of all middle-class mortgages outstanding (line 22), and will bear the risk (through ownership of the underlying mortgages or guarantees of MBSs) of 63 percent of that entire market segment (line 25).

The numbers are even more dramatic if we consider only the conventional/conforming portion of the market. In that case, by the end of 1998, Fannie and Freddie had purchased and retained or guaranteed almost 74 percent of all the conventional/conforming mortgages outstanding (line 26). We project that by 2003 they will have assumed the risk of virtually all these mortgages—91.5 percent. It is no wonder, then, that Fannie and Freddie are advertising their efforts to acquire loans in the subprime categories. They are making a virtue of necessity, since their growth requirements leave them no choice.

Thus, if Fannie remains on the growth path forecast by Franklin Raines and if Freddie keeps pace, by the end of 2003 they will hold in their portfolios more than one-third of all middle-class residential mortgages in the United States (line 22), and more than a quarter (line 21) of all residential mortgages of any kind. Moreover, if we include their guarantees of MBSs, these two companies will be bearing the credit and other risk that is associated with almost half of all the mortgages outstanding (line 24), almost two-thirds of all middle-class mortgages (line 25), and more than 91 percent of all conventional/conforming mortgages (line 26).

In chapter 4 of this study, as those percentages suggest, we show that Fannie and Freddie can meet their growth objectives in the years ahead only by purchasing the riskier loans in the subprime, home equity, and multifamily categories. There will simply not be a sufficient amount of the higher quality, conventional/ conforming mortgages to meet their needs. So in addition to assuming a greater degree of risk simply through their growth over the next four years, the GSEs will also be increasing their overall risk by going more deeply into the lower-quality sectors of the market that until now have been served satisfactorily by nonsubsidized lenders. We explore the nature and possible consequences of the GSEs' growing risk profiles in chapter 6 of this study.

Also, as the GSEs move into the lower-quality market sectors they have previously shunned, they will reduce the portfolio assets, revenues, and profits of thousands of mortgage lenders now active in that market. Although some might think that mortgage lenders will have a choice whether to sell the mortgages they originate to Fannie and Freddie, that is not really the case. Because the GSEs can offer lower government-supported rates for the mortgages they are willing to buy, no lender can offer a competitive rate against another lender who is willing to sell the resulting loan to Fannie or Freddie. Their lower rates also permit Fannie and Freddie to skim the cream from the mortgage markets, leaving other lenders with riskier loans to weaker borrowers. That problem will become more severe as Fannie and Freddie drive deeper into the subprime market.

In other words, if Fannie and Freddie are permitted to continue their growth, even if they don't move outside the secondary mortgage market itself, they will gradually strangle the other participants in the mortgage markets. Those markets will become more concentrated and less diverse than any other financial market in the United States and, increasingly, an obligation of the federal government rather than of the private sector. The impact on competition of Fannie and Freddie's growth is discussed in detail in chapter 5 of this study.

4

Growth

Table 4–1 presents data on the year-to-year growth in the mortgage assets of Fannie Mae and Freddie Mac since 1995. The information for the years 1995 through 1998 is taken from their financial statements; the projections for the years 1999 through 2003 are derived from the assumptions that were used in chapter 3 to project their asset totals for those years.

The data show Fannie and Freddie's growth as a percentage of the *growth* of: (1) the entire residential mortgage market (line 29); (2) the conventional/conforming portion of the market (line 32); and (3) the conventional/conforming plus "all other" portion of the market (line 35).

By presenting the information in that way, we are able to show that, as Fannie and Freddie grow in the year ahead, they will have to drive deeper and deeper into the subprime loan categories in order to find the assets their growth requires. Clearly, Fannie and Freddie cannot continue to grow indefinitely by purchasing and guaranteeing conventional/conforming mortgages. If the conventional/conforming loan market grows at the same rate as the market as a whole in each of the next four years, conventional/conforming mortgages outstanding will increase by $720 billion. But to maintain their projected growth rates, Fannie and Freddie will have to increase their mortgage investments and guarantees by $1 trillion. At the end of 1998, they had retained in their portfolios or guaranteed 74 percent of those loans, and we project that by 2003 they will have retained or guaranteed almost 92 percent.

Thus, beginning in 1998, Fannie and Freddie together, to meet their combined growth goals, were required to add new assets at a rate that exceeded the growth in conventional/conforming mortgages that year. Line 30 of table 4–1 shows that in 1998, the total amount of conventional/conforming mortgage debt outstanding increased by $207 billion. But in that same year, Fannie and Freddie together added $250 billion in new mortgage assets and guarantees to their balance sheets, so that their increase in mortgage credit risk was 121 percent of the net increase in the conventional/conforming market (line 32). By 2003, Fannie and Freddie's need for new assets will equal 146 percent of all net new conventional/conforming loans.

Accordingly, unless they can break into the jumbo market through a change in law, or out-compete Ginnie Mae for a substantial share of the FHA-VA market, the only recourse for Fannie and Freddie is the subprime market.

However, the subprime market, as its name implies, involves considerably greater credit risk than does the conventional/conforming market. By entering that market, Fannie and Freddie will be taking on more risk than they have in the past—risk that may be only partially compensated by the higher interest rates and guarantee fees those mortgages generally yield. We cover that issue more fully in chapter 6.

TABLE 4-1
GROWTH IN RESIDENTIAL MORTGAGES—FANNIE MAE AND FREDDIE MAC VERSUS THE MORTGAGE TOTALS, PAST, PRESENT, AND PROJECTED, 1995–2003
(dollars, in millions)

	History (Year-End)				Projection (Year-End)					Annual Growth Rate: 1995–1998 (%)	Annual Growth Rate: 1998–2003 (%)	Growth Rate Difference
	1995	1996	1997	1998	1999	2000	2001	2002	2003			
27 Annual growth in residential mortgage market—total		227,070	251,517	397,925	373,059	352,541	323,330	342,730	363,294	32.4	-1.8	-34.2
28 Growth in GSE portion		112,742	90,667	250,340	268,210	235,447	234,522	254,420	275,861	49.0	2.0	-47.1
29 GSE portion of total(%)		49.7	36.0	62.9	71.9	66.8	72.5	74.2	75.9			
30 Growth in conventional/conforming—total		118,076	130,789	206,921	193,991	183,321	168,132	178,220	188,913	32.4	-1.8	-34.2
31 Growth in GSE portion		112,742	90,667	250,340	268,210	235,447	234,522	254,420	275,861	49.0	2.0	-47.1
32 GSE portion of total (%)		95.5	69.3	121.0	138.3	128.4	139.5	142.8	146.0			

#	Item												
33	Growth in conventional/conforming & all other mortgages—total		161,945	186,473	338,882	295,077	279,580	256,987	272,915	289,814	44.7	-3.1	-47.7
34	Growth in GSE portion		112,742	90,667	250,340	276,079	236,348	235,420	255,394	276,917	49.0	2.0	-47.0
35	GSE portion of total (%)		69.6	48.6	73.9	93.6	84.5	91.6	93.6	95.5	5.9	5.0	-0.9
36	Nominal GDP—4th quarter	7,529,300	7,981,400	8,453,000	8,947,600	9,394,980	9,864,729	10,357,965	10,875,864	11,419,657			
37	GDP annual growth rate (%)		6.0	5.9	5.9	5.0	5.0	5.0	5.0	5.0			
38	Assumed growth rate after 1998 (%)	5.0											
39	Total mortgages outstanding/GDP (%)	50.3	50.3	50.5	52.1	53.6	54.6	55.1	55.7	56.2			
40	Change in mortgage/GDP ratio (%)	0.6	0.0	0.2	1.7	1.5	1.0	0.5	0.5	0.5			

5

Threat to Private-Sector Competitors

Since Fannie and Freddie are growing faster than the mortgage market itself, their growth comes from taking market share, revenue, and profits from genuinely private-sector mortgage lenders. As shown earlier, to maintain the rate of profit growth on which their stock price depends, Fannie and Freddie must encroach further and further on the private sector. Although they had previously concentrated on the best and most creditworthy loans within the conventional/conforming sector—leaving to the banks, S&Ls, and other nonsubsidized lenders the subprime, home equity, and multifamily loans that represent greater default risks—they are now compelled to wade into that market and begin to take market share from the companies that are already there.

The figures in table 3–2 illustrate quite well the problem that confronts Fannie and Freddie's private-sector competitors. As shown by line 22, the GSEs' share of all residential mortgages (conventional/conforming and "all other") will grow from 19.5 percent at the end of 1998 to almost 36 percent at the end of 2003. That increase of 16.4 percentage points would equal approximately $800 billion, or 12.4 percent of the aggregate principal amount of all mortgages outstanding at the end of 2003. In other words, in four years, $800 billion in principal amount of mortgages—which would otherwise be in the portfolios of private-sector lenders now operating in those markets—will instead be in the portfolios of Fannie and Freddie. That will substantially reduce the mortgage supply for the lenders now in the market, and will force many of them to leave the mortgage lending business entirely.

In effect, the growth of Fannie and Freddie is leading to a steady nationalization of the residential mortgage markets in the United States, without any debate—or even apparent awareness—by Congress.

As shown by lines 29, 32, and 35 of table 4–1, Fannie and Freddie must take most of the growth in mortgages outstanding if they are to meet their market share, revenue, and earnings growth objectives. Since they cannot meet their needs for product solely out of the conventional/conforming mortgages that will come to market between 1999 and 2003, they must look elsewhere for product.

One easy target would be the jumbo market, which will become available if Congress can be induced to eliminate the ceiling on conventional/conforming mortgages. Opening the door for Fannie and Freddie to enter the jumbo mortgage market would, by 2003, give them access to almost $1 trillion of mortgages that are now off-limits.

Other mortgage markets beckon to Fannie and Freddie, including those to be accessed by dipping deeper into the subprime loan pool and assuming the higher credit risks associated with those loans; by expanding more aggressively into the financing of multifamily housing designed for renters, not homeowners; and by acquiring home equity loans in addition to first mortgages. But those can be merely stopgaps. Our projections extend only through 2003; if the growth of Fannie and Freddie continues beyond that year at the rate Frank Raines has forecast, they will at some point acquire all the available residential mortgage product in the United States. As the practical limits of the residential mortgage market are reached, one can easily envision Fannie and Freddie arguing that they should extend their skills and cost advantages into the com-

mercial mortgage market. After all, many office build-
ing and shopping center owners would welcome the
taxpayer subsidy Fannie and Freddie can deliver.

Fannie and Freddie's other opportunity for growth
outside the residential mortgage market is to provide
financial services generally, especially consumer credit
services. Home equity loans, for example, provide a
ready entry into consumer financial services. Once the
GSEs hold a home equity loan, they have the opportunity to use it as a revolving loan fund with which Fannie
and Freddie would be able to supply credit directly to
the homeowner/borrower. Although in one sense that
might be considered loan origination, such a determina-
tion would have to be made by the Department of Housing and Urban Development (HUD)—which in the past
has shown little appetite for challenging Fannie and
Freddie's expansion. If in fact that activity goes unchal-
lenged by HUD, the GSEs could become very large
sources of consumer credit, and through their implicit
government subsidy they would be able to offer consumers better rates than banks and other consumer
lenders.

Perhaps the greatest competitive threat, however,
remains in the mortgage origination process. Although
Fannie and Freddie vigorously deny that they have any
intention to originate mortgages, pointing out that they
lack the statutory authority to do so, what exactly con-
stitutes origination of a mortgage is a matter of inter-
pretation. If Fannie and Freddie were to open their
automated underwriting facilities to direct borrower access over the Internet, it might be possible for them to
provide the prospective homebuyer with a certification
that his or her mortgage would qualify for purchase by
Fannie or Freddie. At that point, the actual lender
would have little to do except to perform the ministerial
acts necessary to fund the loan and deliver it to one or
another of the GSEs. The compensation for that role
would, of course, be small.

In a November 1999 speech to securities analysts, Leland Brendsel, the chairman of Freddie Mac, referred in rather vague terms to major changes in the offing for the mortgage market:

> I can safely predict that within a few short years, the mortgage industry will change dramatically. When the dust settles in the mortgage market, we will be left with an industry structure where investor funds flow to consumers with little drag from antiquated, inefficient processes. Consumers will be able to tap global capital markets at even lower cost than they can today.

And later in the same statement he was even more explicit. Citing the potential of technology "to streamline the entire mortgage process and eliminate inefficiency in the housing finance system," he continued:

> Freddie Mac has brought tremendous efficiency to the mortgage market, but the industry still generates significant costs from redundant operations and expensive transfer of information through all the steps in the mortgage process. As technology wrings out remaining inefficiencies, Freddie Mac's role will be enhanced, as we deliver low-cost funds to consumers even faster and more effectively.

There can be little doubt that Mr. Brendsel was describing a mortgage industry in which, through technology, Freddie Mac would be dealing directly with borrowers and perhaps with consumers generally.

6
Risks

I t is impossible to understand the risks that Fannie and Freddie create for the government and taxpayers without understanding their similarities to the S&Ls that collapsed at the end of the 1980s. Like the S&Ls,

- their principal investments are home mortgages, long-term assets that can abruptly become short-term assets when a home is sold or refinanced;
- they can borrow at government-assisted rates that do not substantially increase as they take on more risk;
- they are unable to manage risk through asset diversification because virtually all their assets are home mortgages.

But Fannie and Freddie are like 1980s S&Ls in another significant way. Scholars reviewing the S&L collapse have shown that it came about in substantial part because the industry was seeking high profits in order to recover the capital depleted by losses during the high-interest-rate period at the beginning of the 1980s. To achieve that profitability, through a process ultimately called "gambling for resurrection," the S&Ls reached for greater and greater risk. Although the debt market usually requires much higher interest rates from companies that are taking on increased risk—if those companies can access the debt market at all—that was not true for the S&Ls. Because their deposits were backed by the government, weak and failing S&Ls were

able to raise the necessary funds to keep on gambling—
ultimately causing immense losses to the government
and the taxpayers.

Of course, Fannie and Freddie are not weak companies, and they have no need to take risks to restore
their capital. But they have strong—indeed, compel-
ling—reasons to continue increasing their profitability.
That circumstance creates the same incentives to take
on risk that the managements of weak S&Ls confronted
fifteen years ago.

The incentives are clear. Fannie and Freddie are
public companies; their shares are listed on the New
York Stock Exchange and are closely monitored by the
investment community. The value that investors place
on their stock at any given moment is not only a vote
on their earnings growth prospects and the quality of
their management, but also directly affects management's compensation. Like the managements of most
large, publicly held companies, the managements of
Fannie and Freddie are compensated in part through
stock options, which in turn acquire increasing value
only if the price of their stock increases.

That creates a strong incentive for the managements of the GSEs, like those of conventional private
firms, to increase their profits and to impress investors
with their potential for profit growth. For example, at
the Merrill Lynch investor conference in September
1999, Fannie Mae chairman Franklin Raines projected
that Fannie Mae would achieve annual earnings growth
of 15 percent in 1999 and over the next four years. But
profit growth at that rate is highly unusual. Fannie already boasts that it is one of only eight companies in
the S&P 500 that can claim to have had a double-digit
rate of earnings growth for twelve straight years. Con-
tinuing that growth in profitability—and indeed increasing it—would be extraordinary for any company in
today's low-inflation environment.

We can only speculate why Mr. Raines would place

such a burden on himself and his management. Possibly it is because he wants to be seen as a highly capable manager, or he feels an obligation to match the success of his predecessors. However, the fact that his compensation and that of the top managers at Fannie Mae are tied to increases in Fannie's stock price also provides a substantial incentive to impress the financial markets.

Once we look at Fannie and Freddie as gigantic S&Ls that are seeking an almost unprecedented rate of profitability growth, we can begin to see why they create risks for the government and the taxpayers that parallel the risks created by the S&Ls in the 1980s. Because of their government backing, they are essentially exempt from debt market discipline—just like the insured S&Ls of the 1980s.

The incentives may be different, but the objectives are the same—to increase profitability by issuing debt at a government-backed rate, while achieving higher profitability through taking on greater risk. In the 1980s, S&Ls tried to do that to replenish their capital; Fannie and Freddie are doing it to maintain the profit growth that sustains a growing market valuation of their stock.

To be sure, Congress has attempted to address the question of GSE risk, using the familiar device of a regulatory agency. In 1991, Congress established the Office of Federal Housing Enterprise Oversight (OFHEO), a regulatory agency charged with supervising the GSEs the way banking regulators supervise banks and S&Ls. Given the experience of the 1980s—not only with the S&Ls but with banks themselves—we should be skeptical about the effectiveness of regulators in controlling the risks of the companies they regulate.

For one thing, there is always the question of asymmetric information—the regulated company knows more than its supervisor about the risks it is taking on. For another, as demonstrated in the case of the S&L industry, the regulated companies frequently have more power to influence Congress than has the regulatory agency, and they are frequently successful in limiting the agency's resources. It is useful to recall that Congress repeatedly supported the S&L industry's efforts to avoid regulatory restriction on its activities. As it happens, in the case of OFHEO, that phenomenon was clearly demonstrated in 1999, when a Senate committee initially capped OFHEO's appropriation at the previous year's $16 million level—despite an administration request for a 20 percent increase. Although an increase to $19 million was ultimately voted, the special effort that was required sent a signal to OFHEO about how much congressional support it will receive if it seriously attempts to control Fannie and Freddie's behavior.

Even without those negative signals, there are good reasons to believe that OFHEO will not act to reduce the GSEs' risk-taking. For example, if Fannie or Freddie's capital ratios slipped too low, OFHEO could direct the troubled GSE to reduce its assets as part of a plan to strengthen its capital position. Shrinkage, however, implies that the GSE in question would sharply reduce its buying and guaranteeing of mortgages. It might even be required to sell assets. That would improve its capital ratios, but the cutback and asset sales could force an increase in mortgage interest rates and a sudden, sharp reduction in housing construction, with secondary effects throughout the economy.

The possibility that there might be severe macroeconomic consequences as a result of an OFHEO regulatory action should raise both systemic-risk concerns about OFHEO's new capital regulations and doubts about the likelihood that they will ever be effectively applied. If OFHEO's capital regulations are believed to threaten severe macroeconomic consequences—and certainly Fannie and Freddie will not be shy about pointing that out—it is easily foreseeable that Congress will act to prevent the enforcement of the regulations.

That example, not at all far-fetched, suggests how difficult it will be for OFHEO to be an effective source of discipline over Fannie and Freddie. And without OFHEO, there is effectively no means of controlling their risk-taking.

Nevertheless, OFHEO *has* proposed a regulation intended to control the riskiness of Fannie and Freddie—including a risk-based capital requirement that imposes capital penalties when risks are not adequately hedged. Undoubtedly, Fannie and Freddie will cite those regulations as a basis for quelling congressional concerns. The question, however, is whether it is reasonable to believe that Fannie and Freddie can achieve the extraordinary rates of growth they are projecting while keeping their risks within tolerable levels. If they do so, they will be unusual companies indeed.

The GSEs' sagging stock prices demonstrate that Wall Street is skeptical on that score. As shown on lines 52 and 55 of table 6–1, both GSEs have experienced a significant decline, per dollar of portfolio investment, since 1995. We project that that trend will continue through 2003. On January 12, 2000, Fannie's common stock closed 20 percent below its twelve-month high, while Freddie closed down a more troubling 28 percent for the same period. That development seems to be puzzling to Fannie Mae chairman Raines, who asked at the Merrill Lynch conference, "So why does the market trade Fannie Mae at a discount to the other companies with similar growth rates?"

There are two possible reasons.

First, some investors may have recognized that Fannie and Freddie are simply running out of room to grow by purchasing the high-quality conventional/conforming mortgages that have been their traditional assets, and that the cost of hedging the risks of lower-quality product may reduce their profitability.

Second, and more ominously, Fannie and Freddie's lagging stock prices may reflect a growing concern in

the equity markets that the GSEs are not adequately
hedging their risks, so that their future earnings may
be hit by losses on the riskier mortgages they are purchasing or guaranteeing today.

In addition to their inherent lack of diversification,
Fannie and Freddie face a number of other risks as
guarantors of MBSs and as holders of large portfolios of
mortgages and MBSs. Those risks include credit risk,
interest-rate risk, counterparty risk, and spread-compression risk, all of which are discussed more fully
below. As we will show, each of those risks can be reduced or hedged, but doing so is costly and will inevita-
bly reduce Fannie and Freddie's profitability. To
compensate for those costs—while trying to maintain
and surpass their past levels of profitability—they must
take on still more risk, always keeping one step ahead
of their regulator.

Credit Risk. In common with all housing lenders, the
GSEs have enjoyed a substantial decline in their credit
losses in recent years. Fannie's pre-tax losses, per mortgage dollar owned or guaranteed, dropped from 5.3
basis points in 1996 to 2.9 basis points in 1998 (table
6–2, line 59); Freddie's pre-tax credit losses dropped
from 10.5 basis points in 1996 to 5.1 basis points in
1998 (line 65).

But the housing market is historically volatile, and
it regularly passes through boom and bust periods related to national economic conditions, interest rates,
and other factors. Completely exogenous factors—an
example might be a change in the tax system that alters
the deductibility of mortgage interest in a significant
way—could have seriously adverse effects, for which
the participants have no effective way to prepare. It is
important to keep in mind that Fannie and Freddie will
be more exposed to the risks of the housing market than
any lenders in history, since their already unprece-

TABLE 6–1

FANNIE MAE AND FREDDIE MAC NET INCOME BY LINE OF BUSINESS, PAST, PRESENT, AND PROJECTED, 1995–2003
(dollars, in millions)

	History (Year-End)				Projection (Year-End)					Annual Growth Rate: 1995–1998 (%)	Annual Growth Rate: 1998–2003 (%)	Growth Rate Difference
	1995	1996	1997	1998	1999	2000	2001	2002	2003			
Net income by line of business (basis points)												
Fannie Mae:												
41 Portfolio investment	1,369	1,694	1,894	1,878	2,219	2,621	2,988	3,346	3,702	11.1	14.5	3.4
42 Credit guarantee	1,003	1,031	1,162	1,540	1,563	1,661	1,770	1,872	1,973	15.4	5.1	−10.3
43 Total	2,372	2,725	3,056	3,418	3,802	4,282	4,758	5,218	5,675	12.9	10.7	−2.3
44 Federal tax rate (%)	28.0	29.5	29.3	25.9								
Freddie Mac:												
45 Portfolio investment	N.A.	785	892	1,021	1,305	1,591	1,857	2,116	2,372	14.0	18.4	4.3
46 Credit guarantee	N.A.	458	503	679	751	760	793	819	841	21.8	4.4	−17.4
47 Total	1,091	1,243	1,395	1,700	2,055	2,352	2,650	2,935	3,213	15.9	13.6	−2.4
48 Federal tax rate (%)	31.2	30.0	29.0	27.8								

Fannie + Freddie:												
49 Portfolio investment	N.A.	2,479	2,786	2,899	3,524	4,212	4,846	5,462	6,074	8.1	15.9	7.8
50 Credit guarantee	N.A.	1,489	1,665	2,219	2,333	2,422	2,563	2,691	2,814	22.1	4.9	-17.2
51 Total	3,463	3,968	4,451	5,118	5,857	6,634	7,409	8,153	8,888	13.9	11.7	-2.2
Net income per $ of business (basis points):												
Fannie Mae:												
52 Portfolio investment		62.8	62.8	51.3	47.0	45.0	43.0	41.0	39.0			
53 Credit guarantee[a]		13.3	14.0	16.9	14.0	13.0	12.5	12.0	11.5			
54 Total		34.0	35.3	35.1	33.6	33.5	33.6	33.4	33.1			
Freddie Mac:												
55 Portfolio investment		63.9	59.0	48.6	44.0	42.0	40.0	38.0	36.0			
56 Credit guarantee[a]		7.9	8.2	10.2	9.5	8.5	8.0	7.5	7.0			
57 Total		21.1	22.3	24.7	26.0	26.3	26.7	26.9	26.7			

a. Assumes no credit risk on GSE/government-guaranteed debt held in portfolio.

N.A. = not available

dented market shares will—as discussed earlier in this study—grow even larger in the future.

Obviously, credit risk is closely related to conditions in the general economy. In recent years, a sustained economic expansion, soon to be the longest in U.S. history, has brought unemployment to record lows while boosting incomes. Both of those factors have led to a steady rise in housing prices. Rising prices in turn have given homeowners more equity in their homes, which protects mortgage lenders and guarantors, notably Fannie and Freddie. However, an economic downturn could depress housing prices while causing a jump in mortgage delinquencies as the unemployment rate rises. Mortgage foreclosures would increase, substantially raising Fannie and Freddie's credit losses.

As Fannie and Freddie are also diving deeper into the pool of subprime mortgages, they will be in largely uncharted waters. Although Fannie and Freddie claim that technology has greatly increased their loan-underwriting capabilities, thereby lowering their risks in subprime lending, that assertion has not been tested by a recession. Further, because of lower down payments from more financially challenged borrowers on properties that may not hold their values well during an economic downturn, losses on subprime lending could be much higher than on higher-quality loans.

Unlike their deep knowledge of and databases on conventional/conforming loans, the GSEs' relative inexperience with the subprime market makes their judgments concerning the risks they are assuming much less sure. Thus, Fannie and Freddie face not only higher likely losses in subprime loans per dollar lent or guaranteed but also greater uncertainty as to how high those losses will be.

To cover their risks in those cases, Fannie and Freddie have in the past relied in part on private mortgage insurance, but recently they have been exploring various devices that would enable them to assume more

TABLE 6–2
CREDIT-RELATED EXPENSES FOR FANNIE MAE AND FREDDIE MAC,
1995–1998

| | | | History (Year-End) | | |
		1995	1996	1997	1998
	Fannie Mae:				
58	Pre-tax credit-related expenses ($, in millions)		409	375	261
59	Pre-tax credit cost (B.P.)		5.3	4.5	2.9
60	Credit guaranty tax rate (%)		31.4	31.1	24.3
61	After-tax credit cost ($, in millions)		281	258	198
62	After-tax credit cost (B.P.)		3.6	3.1	2.2
63	Credit income before credit expense (B.P.)		16.9	17.1	19.1
	Freddie Mac:				
64	Pre-tax credit-related expenses ($, in millions)		608	529	342
65	Pre-tax credit cost (B.P.)		10.5	8.6	5.1
66	Credit guaranty tax rate (%)		28.2	28.4	28.2
67	After-tax credit cost ($, in millions)		437	379	246
68	After-tax credit cost (B.P.)		7.5	6.2	3.7
69	Credit income before credit expense (B.P.)		15.4	14.4	13.9
70	Difference: line 63 − line 69 (B.P.)		1.5	2.7	5.2
	Fannie Mae ($, in millions)	22,200	29,200	43,200	83,600
	% of total portfolio	8.8	10.2	13.6	20.1
	Freddie Mac ($, in millions)	7,665	10,056	12,567	29,817
	% of total portfolio	7.1	7.3	7.6	11.7

B.P. = basis points. 1 B.P. = .01%

Memoranda data—government/GSE securities in portfolio. They presumably have no credit risk.

of the mortgage insurer's risk and thus keep more of the profit for themselves. That is consistent with their desire to increase their profits, but obviously it will also increase their risks of loss in the event of a market turndown.

Finally, Fannie is seeking substantial loan growth in the multifamily housing market, specifically to meet affordable housing goals. Multifamily mortgages can be much riskier than those for owner-occupied, single-family homes, as Freddie learned to its regret a few years ago, because tenant income is more vulnerable to economic downturns and rental property deterioration can be more severe than owner-occupied housing.

Credit-guarantee fees, per dollar of risk assumed, declined during 1999 for both Fannie and Freddie, reflecting lower credit costs as well as increased competition between them for the business of large mortgage originators. A decline in fees is probably only the visible portion of the competition between the GSEs for that business. It is likely that they are also placing their guarantees on MBSs that are backed by somewhat riskier pools of mortgages, for which they are also attempting to assume more of the risk previously taken by mortgage insurers. A sharp and largely unpredictable upswing in credit losses a few years hence could therefore result in substantial losses in their guarantee business.

Interest-Rate Risk. Fannie and Freddie's potential interest-rate risk is growing rapidly as they grow their mortgage portfolios. Those portfolios consist of both whole mortgages and MBSs. In just twenty-one months, from the end of 1997 to September 30, 1999, Fannie increased its mortgage investments by 59 percent, or $188 billion; Freddie's increase was 91 percent, or $150 billion.

Like the S&Ls before them, Fannie and Freddie are heavily dependent on short-term funding to finance the long-term, fixed-rate mortgages they own. That is the classic borrow-short-to-lend-long strategy that S&Ls pursued, with disastrous consequences, when interest rates skyrocketed in the early 1980s. On September 30, 1999, 41 percent of Fannie's debt matured within one year. Freddie was worse off on that date, with 51 percent of its debt due within one year. The two GSEs have tried to lessen their maturity mismatching through various devices, such as callable debt and interest-rate hedging. But such devices are costly, as discussed below, and their extensive use will reduce the GSEs' profitability.

Theoretically, Fannie and Freddie can minimize their interest-rate risk in two ways. First, they can "match fund" their mortgage portfolios. That is, they can sell debt that matches the maturity of their mortgage investments. Maturity matching is complicated, though, by mortgage prepayments, which are not as predictable as risk managers would like. Because the ease and cost of mortgage refinancing have come down in recent years, mortgage prepayments accelerate dramatically whenever longer-term interest rates decline even moderately.

Prepayments create a maturity mismatch because longer-term funding now exceeds longer-term assets. To some extent, Fannie and Freddie can neutralize maturity mismatching by issuing debt that can be called, or repaid, before maturity. But callable debt carries a higher interest rate than noncallable debt, so Fannie and Freddie pay a price for that form of interest-rate risk protection.

The reverse form of interest-rate risk occurs when interest rates rise. In that case, there is likely to be a sharp slowdown in home sales and mortgage refinancing, so that low-rate mortgages remain on the GSEs' books longer than anticipated and have to be supported with higher-rate liabilities. That can result in substantial losses or profit reduction and is exactly what happened to the S&L industry when interest rates spiked in the late 1970s and early 1980s.

Second, Fannie and Freddie have reduced their exposure to higher rates through the use of various financial derivatives, largely interest-rate swaps. That is, for a fee, the two GSEs shift some of their interest-rate risk to third parties. That practice enables them to increase their reliance on cheaper short-term funding.

But derivatives can be costly, particularly when interest-rate volatility causes significant changes in the shape of the interest-rate yield curve.

Counterparty Risk. Hedging interest-rate risk through derivatives raises a separate risk—counterparty risk, which is essentially a form of credit risk. That is, will the counterparty be able to pay when called on to do so under a swap agreement or other form of derivative contract? Counterparty-risk assessment is not a simple process, though, particularly when the counterparty is another financial institution that has entered into many other financial contracts.

The increasing challenge Fannie and Freddie face as they grow larger is finding sufficient counterparty capacity among highly rated potential counterparties: that is, firms with AAA or AA credit ratings. At the end of 1998, 32 percent of Fannie's counterparty risk was with entities rated less than AA; 7 percent of its counterparty risk was with entities rated less than A. Freddie is less forthcoming about its counterparty risk, merely stating that at the end of 1998, its five largest counterparties, which accounted for 60 percent of its total counterparty exposure, were rated at least A+. Consequently, as Fannie and Freddie's risk-hedging needs grow, they may have to pay steadily higher fees for a given amount of protection while relying increasingly on less creditworthy counterparties.

Spread-Compression Risk. In terms of their desire to maintain their profitability, the most serious risk the two GSEs now confront is spread compression: that is, a narrowing of their interest margins. Spread compression has become quite evident at both companies, as reflected in the net income they earn on their portfolio investments per dollar of investment. In 1996, Fannie's net income (excluding the cost of credit risk) per dollar of portfolio investment was 62.8 basis points (table 6–1, line 52); for the first half of 1999, that profit margin had declined to 49.3 basis points. Freddie has experienced a similar reduction—its net income, per dollar of portfolio investment, declined from 63.9 basis points in 1996 (table 6–1, line 55) to 46.6 basis points during the first half of 1999. During the third quarter of 1999, Freddie's interest margin declined seven points from the second quarter, which suggests that its net income per dollar of portfolio investment declined again.

Spread compression is occurring for two reasons. First, as Fannie and Freddie continue to grow, their sheer size and the demands they impose on the financial markets will force up their cost of obtaining credit and interest-rate protection, per dollar of protection obtained.

Second, Fannie and Freddie's purchases of mortgages and MBSs will drive up mortgage prices, thereby reducing mortgage yields, as their mortgage portfolio growth reaches and then exceeds the growth in those portions of the mortgage market where they can lawfully participate. That spread compression will negatively affect Fannie and Freddie's earnings growth and return on equity capital. For Fannie, those data will be found in table 6–1, line 43, and table 6–3, line 85; the comparable data for Freddie are in table 6–1, line 47, and table 6–3, line 100.

Lower mortgage and MBS yields in the face of rising risk-protection costs will squeeze Fannie and Freddie's net interest margins. Unless they can trim their operating costs to fully offset that squeeze, which is unlikely, they will experience even less net income per dollar of portfolio investment. That decline will lower their return on equity capital and slow their earnings growth.

In the face of that inevitable spread compression, Fannie and Freddie's managements will understandably be tempted to take greater risks—specifically, greater credit risk and increased interest-rate risk.

TABLE 6–3
FANNIE MAE AND FREDDIE MAC CAPITAL REQUIREMENTS, PAST, PRESENT, AND PROJECTED, 1995–2003
(dollars, in millions)

		History (Year-End)				Projection (Year-End)					Annual Growth Rate: 1995–1998 (%)	Annual Growth Rate: 1998–2003 (%)	Growth Rate Difference
		1995	1996	1997	1998	1999	2000	2001	2002	2003			
	Fannie Mae:												
71	Core capital (OFHEO-defined)	10,959	12,773	13,793	15,465	18,668	22,109	25,811	29,456	33,602	12.2	16.8	4.6
72	Required minimum capital	10,451	11,466	12,703	15,334	18,168	21,359	24,811	28,456	32,602	13.6	16.3	2.7
73	Core—required minimum	508	1,307	1,090	131	500	750	1,000	1,000	1,000			
74	Mortgage portfolio (net)	252,588	286,259	316,316	415,223	528,811	635,882	754,006	877,960	1,020,492	18.0	19.7	1.7
75	Other assets	63,962	64,782	75,357	69,791	61,007	73,360	86,987	101,287	117,730	2.9	11.0	8.1
76	Total assets on B/S	316,550	351,041	391,673	485,014	589,818	709,242	840,993	979,247	1,138,222	15.3	18.6	3.3
77	Other assets/total assets (%)	20.2	18.5	19.2	14.4	10.3	10.3	10.3	10.3	10.3			
78	Calculated minimum capital: Assets on B/S (2.5%)	7,914	8,776	9,792	12,125	14,745	17,731	21,025	24,481	28,456	15.3	18.6	3.3
79	MBS, other off-B/S (.45%)	2,310	2,467	2,606	2,867	3,060	3,201	3,290	3,406	3,495	7.5	4.0	-3.4
80	Other capital requirement	228	223	305	342	363	427	496	569	652	14.5	13.8	-0.7
81	Other/total capital required (%)	2.2	1.9	2.4	2.2	2.0	2.0	2.0	2.0	2.0			
82	After-tax income for dividends, stock buy-backs, other		911	2,036	1,746	599	841	1,056	1,573	1,529			
83	Net income (%)		33.4	66.6	51.1	15.7	19.6	22.2	30.1	26.9			
84	Dividend payout rate (%)[a]		31.5	30.9	30.9								

#	Item												
85	After-tax return on core capital, before preferred dividends (%)		23.0	23.0	23.4	22.3	21.0	19.9	18.9	18.0			
	Freddie Mac:												
86	Core capital (OFHEO-defined)	5,829	6,743	7,376	10,715	12,229	14,728	17,248	20,019	23,062	22.5	16.6	-5.9
87	Required minimum capital	5,584	6,517	7,082	10,333	11,829	14,228	16,748	19,519	22,562	22.8	16.9	-5.9
88	Core—required minimum	245	226	294	382	400	500	500	500	500			
89	Mortgage portfolio (net)	107,424	137,520	164,250	255,348	337,432	420,329	508,383	605,489	712,419	33.5	22.8	-10.7
90	Other assets	29,757	36,346	30,347	66,073	37,492	46,703	56,487	67,277	79,158	30.5	3.7	-26.8
91	Total assets on B/S	137,181	173,866	194,597	321,421	374,924	467,632	564,870	672,766	791,577	32.8	19.8	-13.1
92	Other assets/total assets (%)	21.7	20.9	15.6	20.6	10.0	10.0	10.0	10.0	10.0			
	Calculated minimum capital:												
93	Assets on B/S (2.5%)	3,430	4,347	4,865	8,036	9,373	11,676	14,122	16,819	19,789	32.8	19.8	-13.1
94	MBS, other off-B/S (.45%)	2,066	2,129	2,142	2,153	2,289	2,352	2,391	2,425	2,455	1.4	2.7	1.3
95	Other capital requirement	89	42	75	145	167	200	236	275	318	17.7	17.0	-0.7
96	Other/total capital required (%)	1.6	0.6	1.1	1.4	2.0	2.0	2.0	2.0	2.0			
97	A-T income for dividends, stock buy-backs, other		329	762	(1,639)	542	(148)	131	164	170			
98	Net income (%)		26.5	54.6	-96.4	26.4	-6.3	4.9	5.6	5.3			
99	Dividend payout rate (%)[a]		26.0	26.5	26.3								
100	After-tax return on core capital, before preferred dividends (%)		19.8	19.8	18.8	17.9	17.4	16.6	15.8	14.9			

a. Common + preferred dividends as a percentage of net income.

B/S = balance sheet.

That temptation is troubling, given their extremely thin capital cushions. Under existing regulations, Fannie and Freddie must have, at a minimum, equity capital (common stock, permanent preferred stock, paid-in capital, and retained earnings) equal to 2.5 percent of on-balance-sheet assets plus .45 percent of outstanding MBS and other off-balance-sheet obligations. The on-balance-sheet capital ratio is one-half the leverage capital ratio required for commercial banks considered to be well capitalized for regulatory purposes. Worse, as is clear from table 6-3, lines 73 and 88, Fannie and Freddie operate much closer to their minimum capital ratio requirement than is generally true for well-capitalized banks, which generally have risk-based capital of 10 percent. Therefore, increased risk-taking, which might not be immediately evident to regulators and stock market analysts, could set up either company—or both—for serious financial difficulties.

Systemic Risk. As Fannie and Freddie continue to grow, they will pose increased systemic risk to the U.S. financial markets. They had $866 billion of debt outstanding as of September 30, 1999. By the end of 2003, that amount will increase by almost $1 trillion, rising to $1.8 trillion (table 6–4, line 105). At that point, or shortly thereafter, the combined debt of the two GSEs may exceed the Treasury debt held by the general public—if budget surpluses continue to shrink the amount of Treasury debt outstanding.

Recently, Fannie and Freddie have been attempting to emphasize the similarity of their debt to Treasury securities, by mimicking Treasury's frequent, regular issuances of new debt. Indeed, at one point Fannie Mae's website contained the statement that its debt securities "will often provide investors with a spread pickup to the Treasury structure." In other words, investors can receive substantially the same security as Treasury debt with an interest-rate premium. If those

TABLE 6-4
FANNIE MAE AND FREDDIE MAC INTEREST-BEARING DEBT OUTSTANDING, PAST, PRESENT, AND PROJECTED, 1995–2003
(dollars, in millions)

	History (Year-End)				Projection (Year-End)					Annual Growth Rate: 1995–1998 (%)	Annual Growth Rate: 1998–2003 (%)	Growth Rate Difference
	1995	1996	1997	1998	1999	2000	2001	2002	2003			
Fannie Mae:												
101 Interest-bearing debt O/S	299,174	331,270	369,774	460,291	560,327	673,780	798,943	930,285	1,081,311	15.4	18.6	3.2
102 O/S debt as percentage of total assets	94.5	94.4	94.4	94.9	95.0	95.0	95.0	95.0	95.0			
Freddie Mac:												
103 Interest-bearing debt O/S	119,328	156,491	172,321	287,234	337,432	420,329	508,383	605,489	712,419	34.0	19.9	−14.1
104 O/S debt as percentage of total assets	87.0	90.0	88.6	89.4	90.0	90.0	90.0	90.0	90.0			
105 Total O/S interest-bearing Fannie and Freddie debt	418,502	487,761	542,095	747,525	897,759	1,094,109	1,307,326	1,535,774	1,793,730	21.3	19.1	−2.2

O/S = outstanding

marketing efforts are successful, actual losses at either of the GSEs—or a perception in the markets of a sudden increase in their riskiness—could result in a serious systemic problem for the economy as a whole.

Despite their efforts to present their securities as substitutes for Treasury securities, Fannie and Freddie are not the Treasury. Their securities are only implicitly backed by the U.S. government; they do not carry the full-faith-and-credit promise of the United States. Indeed, the GSEs' securities are by statute required to state that they are *not* obligations of the United States. They are able to obtain favorable financing because the markets do not believe—given the GSEs' many connections with the U.S. government—that they will be allowed to fail.

But it is important to understand that that condition still leaves some room for doubt. Ultimately the GSEs' ability to fund themselves in the financial markets depends on their ability to manage their risks as well as on conditions in the U.S. housing markets. The housing markets, in turn, are subject to risks—such as changes in the tax code—that cannot be anticipated. An adverse change in the GSEs' financial condition could lead to an increase in the yield spread of the GSEs' debt over Treasury debt. That could be a gradual rise, as the market worries about whether their implicit backing will turn into a bailout, or it could reflect a sudden shift in market perceptions. In the case of Farm Credit System (FCS) debt in 1987, a gradual rise was followed by a sudden tipping point, when the market fled to quality. In the case of the Farm Credit System, the yield spread over longer-term Treasuries went above 100 basis points, signaling that new FCS debt might become unmarketable.[8]

If a similar phenomenon should affect Fannie or Freddie's securities, the financial intermediaries that are currently holding that debt instead of Treasuries may find that they can sell only at substantial losses;

the losses would then raise questions about their own financial stability, and a systemic crisis would arise. To be sure, Congress could resolve the crisis, but a great deal of damage would then have been done to the economy as the market fled to quality and credit sources dried up. The U.S. financial markets experienced that phenomenon during the fall of 1998, in the aftermath of the Russian debt crisis and the Long-Term Capital Management debacle.

Of course, the effect of a Fannie and Freddie crisis would be even more calamitous for the housing markets. If those GSEs were to face substantially higher interest costs in marketing their debt, the costs would be transmitted immediately to the housing market—slowing home purchases and new home construction dramatically. That in itself would have a severely adverse effect on the general health of the U.S. economy.

Fannie and Freddie can contain their risks, but at the cost of reduced profitability. There is no indication in their behavior thus far that they are willing to accept that result.

7
Conclusion

F annie Mae and Freddie Mac are fast becoming a problem that can no longer be ignored. By 2003, they will have assumed the risk—either through ownership or guarantees—of almost one-half of all residential housing mortgages in the United States. In effect, the residential mortgage market will have been partially nationalized, with the taxpayers bearing a risk that should be borne by private stockholders and creditors.

Moreover, we project that in 2003, Fannie and Freddie will own or have guaranteed 91.5 percent of all conventional/conforming mortgages, justifying the concern of private mortgage lenders throughout the United States that they will gradually be squeezed out of their traditional markets, and that Fannie and Freddie are planning to extend their activities to some form of direct relationship with the public.

It seems clear that the problem here is the peculiar structure of Fannie and Freddie—profit-seeking companies that have been granted special status to pursue a public mission. Those objectives are contradictory. Whatever balance Congress initially thought could be achieved between them has been lost.

What are the benefits that Fannie Mae and Freddie Mac claim to provide, and are those benefits worth the cost in taxpayer risk and competition for nonsubsidized mortgage lenders?

Although the GSEs do contribute to liquidity in the mortgage markets, they are no longer necessary for that purpose; private firms now routinely acquire and securitize portfolios of jumbo mortgages—which exceed the size that Fannie and Freddie may purchase—and those private firms could certainly do the same for conventional/conforming loans.

Recognizing the validity of that argument, Fannie and Freddie now claim that their purpose is to reduce middle-class mortgage rates, and point to the fact that those rates are about 30 basis points lower than rates in the jumbo market. However, many economists have noted that that saving for homebuyers is an illusion: the lower interest rate is immediately capitalized into the cost of the home, so that the real benefit of the implicit subsidy goes to developers and homesellers rather than to the homebuyers whom Congress presumably intended to assist.

Weighed against those highly conjectural benefits are the real taxpayer risks that Fannie and Freddie create, and the real danger that they will eventually evict private nonsubsidized lenders from the residential mortgage market.

Policymakers have a number of appropriate potential responses: true privatization of Fannie and Freddie through cutting their links to the federal government; tighter statutory and regulatory restrictions on their efforts to expand their activities; limitations on their use of lobbyists, their political contributions, and their other efforts to manipulate the legislative process; free sale of identical GSE franchises, or the imposition of special taxes, affordable housing burdens, or other costs that would enable the government to recapture their implicit subsidy; forbidding the tying of management compensation to their stock price; and even returning them to their former status as on-budget federal agencies.

Whatever the course ultimately adopted, it is important to recognize that options are foreclosed and solutions become more difficult as Fannie Mae and Freddie Mac continue their de facto nationalization of the residential mortgage market.

Notes

1. In its 1996 report, *Assessing the Public Costs and Benefits of Fannie Mae and Freddie Mac*, CBO concluded that the GSEs reduced interest rates in the conventional/conforming market by passing along about two-thirds of the implicit subsidy they received from the government, while retaining the balance for themselves. CBO estimated that subsidy as $6.5 billion in 1995, a figure that was derived by estimating the GSEs' funding cost savings as a result of their implicit government backing. Prior assessments of the GSEs' credit quality had concluded that, without government backing, Fannie and Freddie would have private-sector credit ratings in the Aa range. That permitted CBO to estimate the savings attributable to the government's implicit credit enhancement by computing the difference between the costs the GSEs would have faced without government backing and the costs they actually paid. That savings was estimated at about 50 basis points for each dollar of funds acquired. CBO then noted that the difference between interest rates in the jumbo market and those in the conventional/conforming market amounted to approximately 35 basis points, and concluded that the GSEs were retaining about 15 basis points, or about one-third of their implicit subsidy.

2. Although Ginnie Mae can borrow at a lower rate than Fannie and Freddie, the GSEs have been able, from time to time, to offer a lower mortgage rate to many subprime borrowers eligible for FHA and VA loans. That may be a consequence of the fact that Fannie and Freddie's MBSs have greater liquidity than Ginnie Mae's, and perhaps shorter duration. It may also be attributable to better underwriting skills at Fannie and Freddie, which might leave Ginnie with higher credit losses. It remains to be seen whether Fannie and Freddie will be able to maintain a permanent beachhead in the FHA/VA market.

3. The limit, which is keyed to housing prices, was $240,000 in 1999.

4. Not to be outdone, in a November 1999 statement to securities analysts, Leland Brendsel, the chairman of Freddie Mac, also pre-

dicted a mid-teens growth in profitability, without specifying the period over which that would occur.

5. In a recent statement, Fannie chairman Franklin Raines divided the residential mortgage market into seven subcategories: conventional/conforming (49 percent), FHA/VA (11 percent), jumbo (19 percent), subprime (6 percent), home equity loans (6 percent), seller-financed (2 percent), and multifamily (7 percent).

6. If Mr. Raines is correct that the jumbo market is 19 percent of the total, that would indicate that Fannie and Freddie have an even larger percentage of the total eligible market.

7. Serious questions arise if Fannie and Freddie are now meeting their growth objectives by purchasing MBSs that are already outstanding in the market. If their purchases of MBSs are made in sufficient amounts to increase prices and decrease yields on outstanding MBSs, then Fannie and Freddie will be reducing the spread between their borrowing costs and the yield they receive on their MBS portfolios. That in itself will raise their risks.

If their purchases do not substantially affect yields in the MBS market, however, it is questionable whether that activity has any salutary effect on mortgage rates for homebuyers. Unless they can show such an effect, Fannie and Freddie will be hard put to explain why that use of subsidized funds qualifies as anything more than a strategy to maintain their targeted earnings growth rate.

Indeed, it seems unlikely that Fannie and Freddie's purchases will appreciably influence MBS market yields. If they reduce homebuyers' interest rates by only about 30 basis points when they transfer two-thirds of their annual subsidy directly into the mortgage markets, the indirect effect of their purchase of outstanding MBSs in the $3 trillion MBS market should be even smaller.

8. Bert Ely and Vicki Vanderhoff, "The Farm Credit System: Reckless Lender to Rural America" (Alexandria, Va.: Ely & Company, Inc., November 1990).

About the Authors

PETER J. WALLISON is a resident fellow at the American Enterprise Institute for Public Policy Research, where he co-directs the Program on Financial Market Deregulation. He has served as general counsel of the U.S. Treasury Department, where he played a significant role in the development of the Reagan administration's proposals for deregulation in the financial-services industry, and as counsel to President Ronald Reagan. He is the author of *Back from the Brink* (AEI Press, 1991) and numerous articles about banking.

BERT ELY is a financial-institutions and monetary-policy consultant. The principal at Ely & Company, Inc., of Alexandria, Virginia, he has specialized in deposit insurance and banking-structure issues since 1981. In 1986, he was one of the first persons to publicly predict a taxpayer bailout of the Federal Savings and Loan Insurance Corporation. He monitors conditions in the banking and thrift industries, the politics of the credit-allocation process, and issues concerning monetary policy and the payments system.